W9-BCO-466

J
595.7
Gan
Ganeri
Insects

788802
17.00

DATE DUE		
MY27 '94		
JY 2 '94		
SE 13 '94		
NO 8 '94		
AP 4 '95		
MY 10 '95		

AN

GREAT RIVER REGIONAL LIBRARY

St. Cloud, Minnesota 56301

GAYLORD MG

Insects

ANITA GANERI

Illustrated by Danny Flynn

FRANKLIN WATTS
NEW YORK • LONDON • TORONTO • SYDNEY

788802

© 1992 Franklin Watts

Published in the United States
in 1992 by
Franklin Watts, Inc.
95 Madison Avenue
New York, NY 10016

Library of Congress Cataloging-in-Publication Data
Ganeri, Anita, 1961–
    Insects / by Anita Ganeri
      p. cm. — (Nature detective)
    Includes index.
    Summary: Examines the habitats, behavior, and life cycles of
various insects, using such physical evidence as eggs and anthills
as starting points for discussion.
    ISBN 0-531-14225-6
    1. Insects—Juvenile literature. [1. Insects.] I. Title.
II. Series: Nature detective (New York, N.Y.)
QL467.2.636 1993   92-7841
595.7—dc20   CIP AC

Designer: Splash Studio
Editor: Sarah Ridley
Additional illustrations: Terry Pastor

Consultants: Many thanks to Michael Chinery,
and Nigel Hester of the National Trust.

All rights reserved.

Printed in Belgium.

The publishers regret that they
have been unable to show the insects
in this book drawn to scale.

Contents

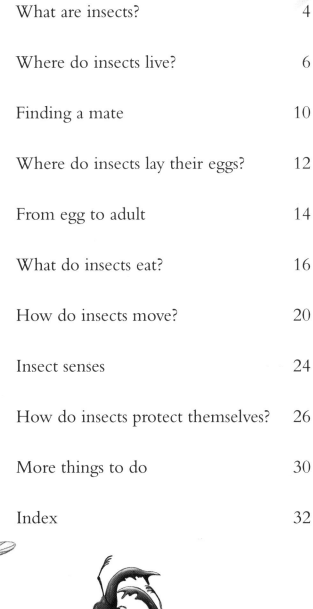

What are insects?

There are more species of insects than all other kinds of animals put together. Over a million species have been identified, but there may be many thousands more waiting to be discovered. Most insects are quite small, but they come in a fascinating range of colors and shapes, from armor-plated beetles to brilliantly colored butterflies. Moths, weevils, flies, bees, ants, and grasshoppers are all types of insect.

Insects belong to the group of animals known as arthropods. They are invertebrates, which means that they have no bones inside their bodies. Instead, their bodies are protected by a hard outer shell, called an exoskeleton. Insects have three parts to their bodies (the head, thorax, and abdomen) and three pairs of jointed legs. Most of them have wings.

Insectlike creatures have been on the earth for hundreds of millions of years. We know from fossils that giant dragonflies with wings up to 30 inches wide appeared on the earth 300 million years ago. These were the largest insects ever known to have lived.

You should be able to see and study insects wherever you live. Once you are familiar with their features and habits, you should also be able to identify the different sorts quite easily.

Arthropods that are not insects

The creatures below are all related to insects, being part of the arthropod group of animals. Can you see why they are not insects? Do any of them have three parts to their bodies, six legs, or wings?

Wood lice and water fleas These are crustaceans, like crabs and shrimps. They have lots more legs than insects and mostly live in water.

Wood louse

Water flea

Centipedes and millipedes These have many more segments to their bodies and many more legs than insects. Centipedes have one pair of legs per segment; millipedes have two.

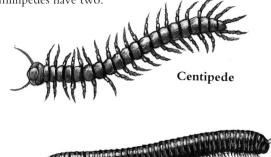

Centipede

Millipede

Spiders, mites, and ticks These are arachnids. They have four pairs of legs and their heads and thoraxes are fused together. They have no wings or antennae. They have small, simple eyes only.

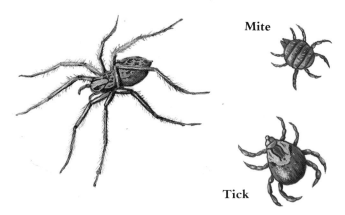

Mite

Tick

Earthworms Earthworms have no legs at all and no hard parts to their bodies.

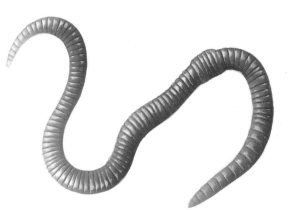

Parts of a bee

Exoskeleton This is made of a hard, tough material, called chitin. It covers all parts of the insect's body. It cannot stretch, so young insects have to molt, or shed, their exoskeleton in order to grow. The exoskeleton is jointed to allow the insect to move. Its muscles are fixed to the inside of the exoskeleton.

Compound eyes These are made up of hundreds of tiny lenses, called facets. Most insects also have tiny simple eyes, called ocelli.

Antennae Antennae vary in size and shape and are useful in sensing vibrations in the air, and smells. They may also be used for hearing and tasting.

Head The head carries the main sense organs (antennae, and compound eyes), and the mouthparts.

Thorax The thorax is divided into three sections. The insect's legs and wings are attached to these sections.

Wings Most insects have two pairs of wings. Flies only have one pair of wings, and some insects have none at all. The size, shape, and number of wings are a good guide for identification.

Waxy coating This keeps the insect waterproof and prevents it from drying out.

Veins The pattern of veins in a wing can also be used to identify a particular insect.

Abdomen The abdomen is usually made up of 11 segments. It holds the insect's heart, digestive system, and reproductive parts. Many female insects have a tubelike organ at the tip of their abdomen called an ovipositor. This is used for laying eggs.

Legs and feet Insects have three pairs of jointed legs. They have claws on their feet and sometimes small pads for gripping.

Sting The bee's sting is actually its modified ovipositor, the organ used for laying eggs. So only female bees can sting.

Spiracle Insects have no lungs, but breathe through a network of tubes, called tracheae, that reach all parts of the body. Air passes through tiny holes in the exoskeleton straight into the tubes. These holes are called spiracles.

Where do insects live?

You should have no problem finding insects to study. They can live almost anywhere! They are found all over the world, even in the hottest, coldest, wettest, and windiest places. They live in fresh water, underground, inside trees, in carpets, and in the smallest cracks or holes. At different stages of their lives (see pages 16-19), insects need different food and environments. So, adults may live on land but their larvae may develop underwater.

Insects have been so successful because they have been able to adapt to changing conditions. They can eat just about anything, and since most of them are quite small, a meager amount of food can feed several insects. Many insects also have special features to help them survive.

Garden insects

Even if you have only a small garden or a window box, it is a good place to start searching for insects. Here are some of the insects you might find to study in the garden.

1 Mining bee Look out for small piles of earth dotted about your lawn. These may be left by mining bees as they dig their nests in the ground. Mining bees are important for pollinating fruit trees.

2 Small white butterfly This butterfly is a common sight in gardens. It lays its light yellow eggs on plants, such as cabbages and nasturtiums. The pale green caterpillars which hatch out feed on the plants and are considered pests by many gardeners. You can easily tell male and female butterflies apart - the male has one black spot and the female two black spots on their forewings.

3 Ladybug The ladybug is a welcome sight in summer gardens, as it feeds on the swarms of aphids which attack plants. Look out for different patterns and numbers of spots on the ladybug's back.

**4 Spittlebug 5 Tortoiseshell butterfly
6 Aphid 7 Earwig**

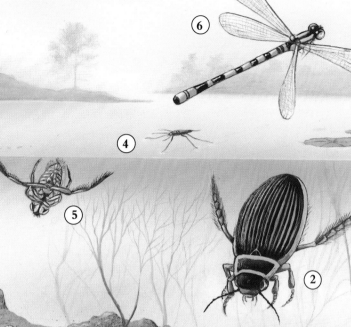

Pond and river insects

Slow-moving or still water is one of the best places to look for insects. You'll find them above and below water, on plants' leaves and stems, or flying and darting about in the air. The best time to look is in the early morning. The insects haven't had time to warm up in the sun and are less active and easier to spot.

1 Whirligig beetle These insects feed on mosquito larvae or dead insects on the water surface. They whirl around and around on the surface, often in groups. They dive quickly if they are startled.

2 Great diving beetle This beetle stores air under its tough wing cases for use when it dives. It comes up tail-first to get a new air supply. It has huge jaws and is a fierce predator. Its larvae live underwater.

3 Rat-tailed maggot This maggot is the larva of the drone fly. It lives in shallow, stagnant water. It breathes through its 6-inch-long tail, which reaches to the surface like a submarine periscope.

**4 Water strider 5 Water boatman (backswimmer)
6 Damselfly**

AMAZING FACTS

Small wingless moths living in Antarctica can survive temperatures as low as –40°F. They have substances, such as glycerol, in their blood which act as antifreeze.

Fog-drinking beetles live in the hot, dry Namib Desert. They have an amazing way of collecting water. At night, they stand, heads down, facing the wind. As fog rolls in off the sea, it condenses on the beetles' backs and trickles down to their mouths.

The Helophorus beetle breeds only in water-filled hoofprints along the edges of woodland.

Petroleum fly larvae live in pools of crude oil in California. They breathe through a tube to the surface. They live on other insects trapped in the sticky oil.

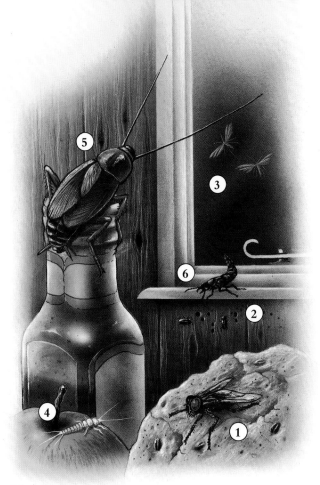

Insects in the home

Your house may be home to many different kinds of insects, from carpet beetles to moths fluttering around the light bulb. These are some of the other, common insects you might find.

1 Housefly Houseflies are unwelcome visitors in the home because they can easily spread diseases. They breed on garbage and animal dung. They can carry germs into the home and onto any food they land on.

2 Furniture beetle Small, round holes in the woodwork are tell-tale signs of furniture beetles. The beetles lay their eggs in wood. The larvae, called woodworm, burrow through the wood for up to five years. Then the adults chew their escape holes through the wood to the outside.

3 White plume moth These delicate moths are attracted to lights on inside the house. You may see them fluttering against the windowpane.

4 Silverfish 5 Cockroach 6 Devil's coach-horse

Field and meadow insects

A great many insects live in fields and meadows. The plants provide them with food, security, and places to lay their eggs. The best time to look for these insects is in spring and summer.

1 Meadow grasshopper This grasshopper is usually green, but it can also be brown. It likes to sunbathe on grass stalks. Groups of these grasshoppers sing together, sounding like sewing machines.

2 Click beetle This beetle's larvae, called wireworms, are very destructive. They attack the roots of spring and autumn crops. The adult beetles are nocturnal. They shelter among plant roots during the day.

3 Honeybee Honeybees are highly social insects, living in huge colonies of as many as 50,000 individual bees. In the wild they may nest in hollow trees. Worker bees visit summer flowers, pollinating them and collecting nectar with which to make honey.

4 Painted lady butterfly 5 Dung beetle

Woodland insects

You will find plenty of insects in woodland. Here are some of the insects you might see in and around an oak tree.

1 Oak gall wasp These small, antlike creatures lay their eggs in the buds, roots, or leaves of oak trees. When the eggs hatch, a swelling grows around the grubs. Look out for these swellings, called galls.

2 Stag beetle These large beetles live in tree trunks and old, rotten stumps. They are named after their antlerlike jaws. The male may grow up to 3 inches long.

3 Wood cricket This small cricket lives among leaf litter on the ground in woodlands. It is most active on warm days when it runs and jumps about. You may hear the male's warbling song on warm evenings.

4 Red admiral butterfly You may see these butterflies visiting woodland flowers.

Insect watching

Because many insects are small and quick moving, they can be difficult to spot. Many are also well camouflaged among leaves or on bark. A few pieces of equipment, and lots of patience, will help you to find them more easily. Always remember to leave habitats as you find them, replacing any stones or logs you move.

Field guide A good field guide will help you to identify many of the insects you will see.

Notebook and pencils Rough sketches of insects can be very useful (see page 30). You should also note down where and when you saw the insect, what the weather was like, and what the insect was doing. Note any special features, such as color, wing shape, and size.

Hand lens A hand lens is important for looking at insects in detail. Use one with a magnification of x 10. Hang the lens on a cord around your neck so you don't lose it.

White bed sheet or paper (umbrella) Place the bed sheet or paper under a bush and shake the bush hard so any insects fall onto the sheet. You could also catch them in an umbrella, hung open from the branch of a tree.

Clear plastic containers If you want to collect insects for a closer look, put them in a clear plastic container with a bit of grass or some leaves. Try not to handle them too much – they are very fragile. Sketch or identify them, then let them go.

Pooter A useful instrument for catching small insects from leaves, twigs, and bark. It is made of a plastic or glass jar with two tubes (one long and one short) inserted in the lid. See page 30 for more about pooters and how to use them.

Finding a mate

An adult insect's life may be very short. During that time, however, it has to find a mate. Then the female can lay her eggs (see pages 12-13). Competition to find a suitable mate is often very fierce. There may also be other problems to overcome, such as bad weather, a long distance to cover, or few other insects of the same species surviving. Many male insects use colors, lights, scents, and different ways of flying to attract females.

Mating usually takes place in warm weather, in spring or summer. Look out for differences in size and color between the males and females of many species. You can check these in your field guide.

Emperor moths Most moths rely on special scent chemicals, called pheromones, to attract a mate. (There is more about pheromones on page 25.) Female emperor moths give off such a strong scent that males can smell it over a mile away. They pick up the scent with their feathery antennae. These smells cannot be detected by human noses.

Stag beetles Stag beetles use their huge, antlerlike jaws in the same way that real stags use their antlers – to fight off rival males and defend their breeding sites. The beetles lock antlers and try to throw each other over.

Empid flies Empid flies feed on other insects, including each other. When the male goes to mate, he runs the risk of being eaten by the female. To distract her attention away from him, he takes her a gift of a small insect wrapped in silk. While the female eats the insect, they mate.

Glow worms Look out for sparkling patches of grass at dusk. The greenish lights are made by female glow worms. They cannot fly but rest on the grass, signaling to any males flying overhead. The females make the lights with their tails. Males have large eyes to pick up the lights in the dark.

Dragonflies Some male dragonflies choose a stretch of riverbank or pond shore as their own territory. They defend their territory fiercely, patrolling it and chasing away rivals. They mate in an unusual way, forming a heart shape.

Deathwatch beetles These beetles lay their eggs in timber, where they are a serious pest. The adults appear in spring. To attract mates, they tap their heads against wood.

Butterflies Butterflies are first brought together by color patterns and ways of flying. When European grayling butterflies are ready to mate, the male bows to the female. Then he clasps her antennae in his wings and brushes scent onto them.

Praying mantis

In some species of praying mantis, the female is famous for eating her mate during or after mating. The female has specially adapted front legs for grasping prey, usually other insects. During mating, she may use them to grip the male. She starts eating at his head and works her way down. The male makes a good meal and also helps to nourish the eggs which the female will lay. The male does try to avoid his fate, by keeping out of the way of the female's grasping forelegs during mating.

Where do insects lay their eggs?

After mating, most female insects lay eggs which will grow into new adults (see pages 14-15). Females are very fussy about where they lay their eggs. Most butterflies, for example, will lay only on a particular species of plant, in the right conditions.

Insects lay their eggs in a huge variety of places: on plant stems or leaves, in water, on the ground, on animals, or inside other insects. The site is chosen to give the young insects a good supply of food and a chance of survival. Look out for clusters of eggs on the underside of plants' leaves and for the different shapes and colors of the eggs.

Orange-tip butterfly Female orange-tip butterflies usually lay their eggs on the flowers of sweet rocket, honesty, and other plants in the *Crucifer* family. Sometimes they lay them on the stalk. The oval-shaped eggs are white to start with, but turn orange after a couple of days have passed.

Spider wasp Spider-hunting wasps lay their eggs in underground burrows. The female wasp paralyzes a spider with her sting and then digs a burrow in which she buries it. She then lays a single egg on top of the spider and covers the hole. When the grub hatches, it has fresh spider meat to feed on.

AMAZING FACTS

A queen termite grows over a hundred times bigger than the other termites. She can lay as many as a thousand eggs a day, and can lay more than one a minute.

Some giant water bugs lay their eggs on the male's back. He acts as a nursemaid until the eggs hatch.

The potter wasp lays its eggs inside delicate pots of mud and clay. It lays one egg in each pot and adds a store of caterpillars for the newly hatched larva to feed on.

Earwigs Most insects lay their eggs, then leave them to hatch. Female earwigs, however, watch over their eggs and regularly wash them to prevent them from getting moldy. The white eggs are laid in a small hole in the ground. Even when they hatch, the mother stays with the young until they are old enough to fend for themselves.

Leaf miners Leaf miner flies lay their eggs inside or underneath leaves. When the eggs hatch, the larvae make tunnels inside the leaf as they feed. These tunnels show up as yellow or brown lines, or blotches, on the leaf's surface.

Mosquitoes Mosquitoes lay their eggs as they fly over water. Groups of eggs float on the surface like rafts.

Nests and hives

Some insects build elaborate nests where they lay their eggs and raise their young. These are usually social insects, such as bees, wasps, and ants, which live in large colonies.

Wood wasps and ichneumon flies Wood wasps, or horntails, have long ovipositors at the tips of their abdomens. The wasps use their ovipositors to drill into pine tree trunks and lay their eggs under the bark. The eggs can take up to three years to hatch.

Ichneumon flies are parasites. The female of one species lays her eggs on the larvae of wood wasps, using her long ovipositor. The insect may use its sense of smell to locate the larvae under the tree bark.

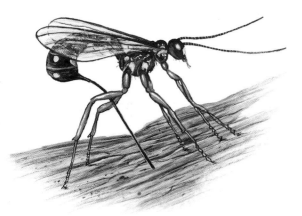

Wood ants Keep a lookout for anthills on the forest floor. These are made by wood ant They build domes of leaves and twigs over their nests. A large nest may contain over 100,000 ants. Among them are several queen ants, who lay the tiny, white eggs.

Bees Inside a hive, the queen bee lays her eggs in six-sided cells made of wax. She lays one egg in each cell. When the egg hatches, the grub is fed with honey and pollen. Then the cell is sealed up with more wax. The larvae develop into adult bees which bite their way out through the wax lid of the cell.

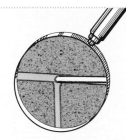

Solitary wasps and egg-laying

You can encourge solitary wasps to lay eggs in your garden, by drilling some small holes in some bricks or logs located in a sunny, but sheltered position. Get an adult to help you with this. In early spring, take a bundle of clear drinking straws and block one end with modeling clay. Stick the modeling clay ends into the holes and leave them there. From time to time, remove the straws carefully and check for any signs of nest-building or egg-laying.

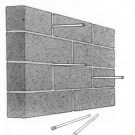

From egg to adult

Many insects go through amazing changes in their bodies as they move from eggs to adults. This process is called metamorphosis. Insects such as butterflies and moths undergo

Complete metamorphosis

"complete" metamorphosis. They change from eggs into larvae (in this case, caterpillars), then into pupae before finally emerging as adults. Insects such as grasshoppers, dragonflies, and cockroaches undergo "incomplete" metamorphosis. They turn from eggs into young, called nymphs, then into adults.

2. The caterpillars spend their time feeding and growing. As they get bigger, they have to molt their skin and grow a new, larger skin. This usually happens four times.

1. The female red admiral butterfly lays her greenish, barrel-shaped eggs on nettle leaves. They take about a week to hatch into caterpillars, the larvae of butterflies.

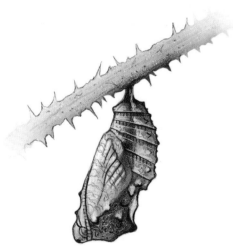

3. Then each caterpillar turns into a chrysalis, or pupa, hanging from a nettle leaf or stalk. Inside the chrysalis, the caterpillar's body breaks down completely and reforms as an adult insect.

4. After two or three weeks, the chrysalis splits open and an adult butterfly struggles out. At first, its wings are crumpled and soft. They gradually expand and harden as blood flows through their veins.

Incomplete metamorphosis

1. Dragonflies lay their eggs in water. It may take up to three years for the adult insects to finally emerge.

2. The eggs hatch into nymphs, which live underwater and breathe through gills, like fish. They are fierce predators.

3. The nymphs molt over ten times, gradually looking more and more like adults.

4. When the adult is ready to emerge, the wingless nymph climbs up a plant stalk out of the water. Its skin splits and the winged adult appears. Look out for discarded skins around the edges of ponds.

Watching metamorphosis

To watch how butterflies metamorphose, collect a leaf which has some eggs of red admiral, monarch, or small white butterflies stuck on it. The best time to find these is in May or June.

Put the leaf on a piece of blotting paper inside a box with a tight-fitting lid. Look every day to see if the eggs have hatched.

Then transfer the caterpillars to a large cardboard box, with a piece of plastic cling wrap taped to the front so you can see inside. Punch some small holes in the sides of the box for ventilation. Inside the box, stand some of the caterpillars' plant food in a jar of water. (You can find out what they eat from your field guide.) Remember to check that the food and water supply doesn't run out.

Keep a close watch as they change into pupae and eventually turn into adults, which may not happen until the following year. Set the adult butterflies free as soon as you can.

What do insects eat?

Many insects eat different foods at different stages of their development. Some species have carnivorous (meat-eating) larvae, for example, but herbivorous (plant-eating) adults. The amount they eat at each stage also varies (see pages 16-19). Many adult insects hardly eat anything at all. Their energies are concentrated in finding a mate and breeding.

An insect's diet depends on where it lives and any special adaptations it has for feeding. Many insects feed on plants, including leaves, stems, flower pollen, wood, and nectar. Other insects eat blood, carrion, and each other. Look out for tell-tale holes in the leaves of your garden plants, in fruit, and even in wooden furniture inside your house. Try to work out which insects have been feeding on them.

How do insects eat?

Insects have different types of mouths and jaws, depending on the food they eat and the way that they eat it. There are two main methods of feeding: sucking, or biting and chewing. Insects have several kinds of jaws which are adapted to tackle particular types of food.

Red admiral butterfly Butterflies and moths suck up liquid nectar with a long, hollow tube, called a proboscis. This is coiled up when not in use. Red admiral butterflies have very long proboscises. They use them to feed on over-ripe apples in autumn gardens. As the fruit ripens, it ferments and produces alcohol. The butterflies get quite drunk as they feed. They fall over and cannot fly properly until the effect of the alcohol wears off.

Housefly Part of the housefly's jaw forms a spongy pad for sucking up liquids. Houseflies can carry and spread over 30 diseases, such as cholera, typhoid, and even leprosy. They breed on animal dung and rotting household garbage. If they then land on uncovered food in the house, they can easily transmit disease-carrying bacteria.

Tiger beetle Beetles have powerful, external jaws for biting and chewing their food. Adult tiger beetles feed on ants and other small insects.

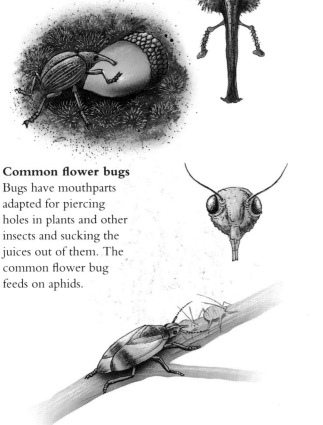

Nut weevil Weevils are beetles with long snouts, called rostrums. These have small, biting jaws at their tips. Most weevils, in both larval and adult forms, eat plants. The female nut weevil uses her snout to bore a hole into hazel nuts and acorns, then lays her eggs inside. The larvae feed on the inside of the nut.

Common flower bugs Bugs have mouthparts adapted for piercing holes in plants and other insects and sucking the juices out of them. The common flower bug feeds on aphids.

What do larvae and nymphs eat?

Adult insects usually lay their eggs on plants or in places where there is plenty of food for the newly hatched larvae and nymphs. The larvae and nymphs are specialized for feeding.

Crane flies Crane fly larvae live in muddy stream beds or in damp ground. Most of them scavenge on decaying matter. The brownish gray larvae have such tough skins that they are known as "leather-jackets."

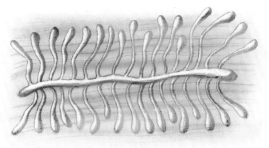

Bark beetles Adult bark beetles mate under the bark of trees, such as oak, chestnut, elm, pine, and spruce. The female tunnels between the bark and underlying wood, producing "galleries" as she goes. She lays her eggs in these "galleries." When the larvae hatch, they chew their way through the wood and create side tunnels. The pattern of tunnels can help identify the different species of bark beetles.

Caddis flies The larvae of caddis flies live underwater, in rivers and streams. Many species protect their bodies with cases of silk, strengthened with grains of sand and small stones. Some also spin tiny nets, suspended between plants or stones, and facing upstream. These trap scraps of plant or animal food for the larvae to eat.

Insect diets

Here are some examples of insect diets and the different ways that insects have of collecting their food.

Bumblebee Bumblebees visit flowers to feed on nectar and collect pollen. They pack the pollen grains into bristly "baskets" on their hind legs. They can then carry it back to their nests where it is used to feed the young bees. Bumblebees play a crucial part in pollinating flowers.

Mosquito Mosquitoes use their long mouthparts for sucking blood. It is only the females who feed on blood, however. The males drink nectar. You can tell the males by their bushy antennae.

Cockroach Cockroaches eat anything they can find. These scavengers usually live on the ground and feed on dead or decaying plants. However, they are also pests in the home, eating anything from food scraps to household garbage.

Darter

Hawker

Dragonfly Adult dragonflies are skillful, agile hunters which catch their insect prey in midair. Darters are dragonflies which perch above the water and dart out at prey. Hawkers "hawk" up and down above the water.

Burying beetle These beetles feed on and lay their eggs on the dead bodies of animals, such as birds and mice. They bury the bodies in the ground, and the larvae feed off the rotting meat or the other scavenging insects feeding there.

Robber fly These predators perch on lookout posts, then pounce on other insects as they fly past. Then they suck out their juices. Robber flies have hairy faces which help protect their eyes from their prey.

Feeding butterflies

One of the best ways of watching butterflies feed is to create your own butterfly garden. The best plants to grow to attract day-flying insects are buddleia, lavender, red valerian, ice plants, honesty, aubretia, wallflowers, and sweet rocket. All these produce plenty of nectar. For moths and night-flying insects, choose plants such as evening primrose, phlox, honeysuckle, and night-scented

stock. These all flower at night. Watch regularly to see how many butterflies and moths they attract.

How do insects move?

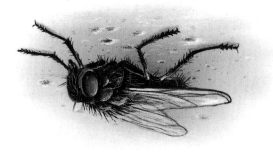

Insects have various ways of moving to find food and escape from danger. Some move a great deal. Others hardly move at all. The young spittlebug stays in the same spot sucking food out of the food plant, hidden under its "cuckoo spit." Some bugs and burnet moths with warning colors don't move about much either.

Many insects have special adaptations to help them move. Long legs are good for walking, running, or jumping. Strong, broad forelegs are ideal for digging and swimming. Most insects also have wings for flying. Watch out for these features and the way they are used.

Water strider The surface of water is covered in a thin, fragile skin. Water striders are adapted for walking over water. They have pads of wax-coated hairs on their four back legs which repel the water and stop them sinking.

Housefly Have you ever wondered how houseflies are able to walk upside down on ceilings without falling off? This is because they have hairy, sticky pads on their feet, between their claws. These are strong enough to grip even the smoothest surface.

Grasshopper Grasshoppers and crickets have long hind legs for jumping. To escape predators, they straighten their legs and launch themselves into the air. Some grasshoppers can leap about 20 times the length of their bodies.

Water boatman The water boatman has a broad fringe of hairs on its hind legs, which it uses as oars. It lives underwater and swims on its back using its hind legs.

Click beetle If a click beetle falls off a twig and lands on its back, it has a dramatic way of righting itself. It arches its body backward until just its head and tail are touching the ground. Then it suddenly lets go and springs into the air, with a clicking sound. It may have several goes before it lands the right way up.

Red ant Ants have long, thin legs for walking and running. When insects walk, they put down one leg on one side and two legs on the other. Keeping three legs on the ground at once helps them to balance.

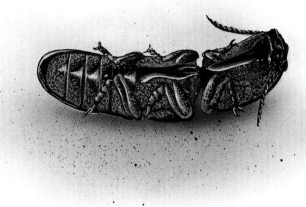

Caterpillar Most caterpillars have three pairs of true legs and five pairs of false legs. They use their true legs for holding food and walk by moving each pair of false legs in turn.

Looper caterpillar The moths of the Geometridae family have caterpillars called "loopers." These caterpillars have only two pairs of false legs. They walk by moving their hind legs forward, so that their body forms a loop. Then they move their front legs forward to flatten their body out.

Looking at wings

You can identify insects by their wings. When you see an insect, look at it carefully. Does it have wings and what shape are they? How many pairs? Does it have hard wing cases? What color are the wings, and do they have any special markings, such as eye spots? What pattern do their veins make?

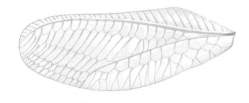

Watch insects in the air. How do they fly? Do they hover, flap their wings, or glide? How fast do they flap their wings? A butterfly flaps its wings about 12-20 times a second, a fly 100-200 times a second, and a honeybee 250 times a second.

Wings and flying

Most adult insects have wings and can fly. Insect wings come in a wide variety of shapes, colors, and sizes. They are strengthened by a network of hollow tubes, called veins. These veins are made of strong chitin, as is the exoskeleton. The pattern of veins is an important guide to identification. Insects use muscles in the thorax to flap their wings.

Lacewing

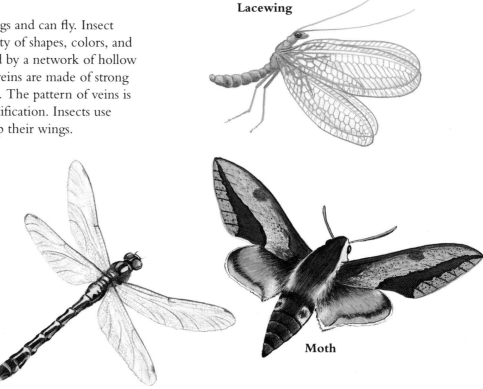

Insects with two pairs of wings Most insects have two pairs of wings. They include dragonflies, lacewings, caddis flies, butterflies, moths, bees, and wasps. When moths, bees, and wasps are flying, their two pairs of wings are held together by tiny hooks and catches. Dragonflies move all four wings independently. They can hover and even fly backwards.

Dragonfly

Moth

Insects with hard wing cases The front wings of beetles and bugs have become adapted as hard wing cases, to protect the body and the back wings. The back wings are folded under the wing cases when not in use. The wing cases are held out to let the insects fly. The wing cases of some beetles, such as ladybugs, are brightly colored. You can use these colors for identification.

Hoverfly

Insects with one pair of wings Flies, including houseflies, hoverflies, crane flies, and mosquitoes, have only one pair of wings. Instead of back wings, these flies have two small knobs, called halteres. These help a fly to balance in the air when it is being buffeted by the breeze.

Crane fly

Ladybug

Cockchafer

Insects with no wings

Insect larvae, such as grubs, maggots, and caterpillars, do not have wings. Some adult aphids and ants also lack wings although some winged ants appear in summer. These are the ones that will mate.

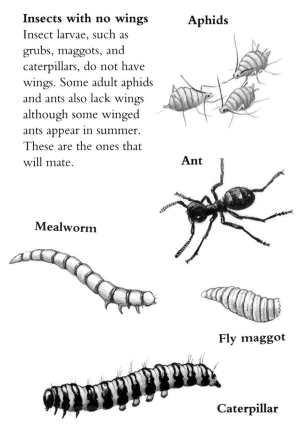

Aphids

Ant

Mealworm

Fly maggot

Caterpillar

Dancing bees

Honeybees perform a special dance on their honeycombs, in order to tell each other where to find food. A worker that has found a good supply of nectar returns to the hive and begins to dance over the combs in a figure 8. The faster the dance, the nearer the food is. The speed and direction of the dance show the other workers where they can find the nectar.

AMAZING FACTS

Despite their small size, many insects make incredibly long migratory flights. Each year, monarch butterflies leave their breeding grounds in North America and fly some 2,000 miles south to Mexico and California. Here they spend the winter, roosting on pine and fir trees. One site in Mexico is thought to be visited by over 14 million butterflies, crowded into a small space.

According to the laws of physics, a bumble bee should not be able to fly. Its body is too big for its wings.

The common flea can jump up to 13 inches along the ground, over 200 times its own length. The longest human jump is not even five times a human's height. The flea can also jump nearly 8 inches high, about 130 times its own height. For its size, the flea can jump longer and higher than any other animal.

The Queen Alexandra's birdwing butterfly is the largest butterfly in the world. Females may have wingspans of over 11 inches.

A tiny midge, called Forcipomyia, beats its wings over 62,000 times a minute, faster than any other insect.

Insect senses

Insects cannot sense the world around them in the same way that we do. They do not have sense organs such as noses or proper ears, for example. Instead, other parts of their bodies are used for sensing things. They smell, taste, and feel things with their antennae. They can also sense things, such as vibrations in the air, with the hairs on their bodies.

We don't know exactly what insects can see, hear, or understand of the world around them. We do know that some of their senses, for example, their sense of smell, are much more acute than our own.

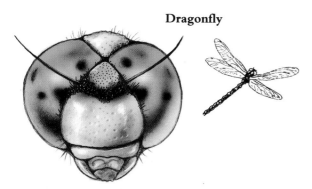

Dragonfly

Eyes Insects have two types of eyes – simple and compound. Most have three simple eyes, or ocelli, arranged in a triangle on the top of their head. They are probably used for sensing different amounts of light.

Insects also have a pair of large, compound eyes. These are made up of tiny lenses, called facets. Compound eyes are superb at judging distances and seeing small movements. The more lenses the insect has, the smaller the movements it will be able to see. A dragonfly may have as many as 28,000 facets in each eye.

Tastebuds Butterflies, bees, and many flies taste things with their feet. If they land on something that tastes sweet, they will immediately start to feed on it.

Bluebottle

Hairs for feeling The hairs on an insect's body are very important for sensing things. These are not true hairs; they are made of chitin, the same substance which builds the exoskeleton. They are connected to the main nerves inside the insect's body.

The hairs can sense vibrations in the air, so that insects such as bees know which way the wind is blowing and caterpillars can curl up in a defensive posture if they sense another creature approaching. Cockroaches and other insects have fine, hairlike feelers at the ends of their abdomens. These are called cerci and are sensitive to touch.

Cricket

Tympanum

Ears Insects do not have ears on their heads and, in fact, most probably cannot hear at all. Grasshoppers and crickets, however, use song to attract mates and need "ears" to pick up these sounds. Crickets have ears on their forelegs. The ears are small membranes, called tympana. These pick up sound waves in the air, as our eardrums do. Grasshoppers have ears on the sides of their bodies.

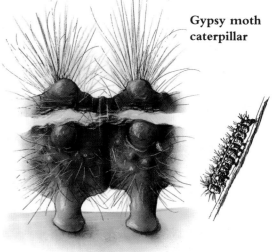

Gypsy moth caterpillar

Antennae

Insects use their antennae for smelling, touching, and even tasting. The antennae tell the insect about its surroundings. An insect's most important and most acute sense is that of smell. It is particularly important because insects communicate using special chemicals, called pheromones, which usually take the form of smells. They are used to attract mates (see page 10), sound the alarm, lay trails to food, and so on.

An insect's antennae are its most important sense organs. Many moths have feathery, branched antennae. This gives them a large surface area, increasing their ability to detect smells, even at a distance. Antennae come in a wide range of shapes and sizes, which will help you to identify various insects. For example, butterflies have clubbed antennae; crickets have long, fine antennae and some beetles have fan-shaped antennae.

Most insects have some way of keeping their antennae clean and in good working order. Bees and some beetles have a special hook on their forelegs for cleaning their antennae.

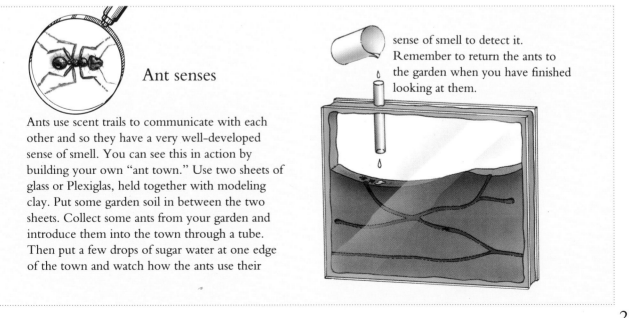

Ant senses

Ants use scent trails to communicate with each other and so they have a very well-developed sense of smell. You can see this in action by building your own "ant town." Use two sheets of glass or Plexiglas, held together with modeling clay. Put some garden soil in between the two sheets. Collect some ants from your garden and introduce them into the town through a tube. Then put a few drops of sugar water at one edge of the town and watch how the ants use their sense of smell to detect it. Remember to return the ants to the garden when you have finished looking at them.

How do insects protect themselves?

Insects have many enemies. Most of these are predators, such as birds and other animals, for whom insects are a major part of their diet. An insect spends a good part of its life avoiding the hungry mouths of its enemies.

Insects have developed many ways of escaping from danger. Most fly, run away, or hide in cracks and crevices. Others have weapons, such as stings or poisons. Some use colors to warn predators off, to show that they taste horrible, or to camouflage themselves and escape attention.

Stings Bees and wasps have long, hollow stings for injecting poison into their enemies. A honeybee's sting is barbed. If it stings you, it cannot pull its sting out again and the bee dies. Wasps and hornets have smooth, unbarbed stings. They can pull their stings out and use them again. Stings are the modified ovipositors (egg-laying organs) of female insects (see page 13).

Formic acid Many species of ants can inflict painful bites or stings on potential predators. Others have the ability to squirt their attackers with stinging formic acid, firing it from the tips of their abdomens.

"Cuckoo spit" You can easily see where spittlebug nymphs are by the frothy mass of white bubbles they secrete around themselves on plant stems. This is known as "cuckoo spit." It helps to protect the nymphs from being eaten and from drying out in the sun. Look out for the froth in springtime in your garden.

Piercing jaws Backswimmers, or water boatmen, swim on their backs in ponds. They are fierce carnivores (meat-eaters) and will attack tadpoles and small fish. In self-defense, they will also pierce the skin of enemies with their needlelike jaws.

Armor plating Many adult beetles have heavy armor plating to protect their bodies. The armor is made of their front wings. These are hard and horny to protect the delicate hind wings used for flying. The front wings also help reduce the amount of precious moisture lost from a beetle's body.

Poison gas Bombardier beetles have an unusual but effective way of putting off predators. If an enemy approaches, the beetle covers it in a cloud of hot, poison gas. The gas is made inside the insect's abdomen, from two harmless chemicals. As they mix, they produce a sudden, explosive sound.

\\\\\\\\\\\\\\\\\\\\||||||||||||||||//////////////

AMAZING FACTS

Some insects are considered pests by farmers whose crops they attack or by people whose homes they invade. Others are very useful, helping to protect the crop from other harmful pests.

The caterpillars of the silkworm moth produce silk which is woven into cloth. The silk comes from the cocoons spun by the caterpillars before turning into pupae.

Insects can be used as pest controllers. Small moths called *Cactoblastis* were used to control the spread of prickly pear cacti in Australia.

/////////////||||||||||||||||||\\\\\\\\\\\\\\\\\\

Winter sleep

Many insects hibernate as larvae or as adults. By spending the winter asleep, they avoid the harsh weather and the lack of food. Others protect themselves from the cold by migrating to warmer places. Look out for insects hibernating in your garden, but don't disturb them.

Comma butterfly
These butterflies hibernate in October, in gardens, woods, and parkland. They cling to tree branches, bushes, or dead leaves and close their wings so that they look like dead leaves. They wake in spring to pair up and breed.

Herald moth Herald moths often hibernate inside houses or hollow trees or among woodpiles. They hibernate from October to spring. They look like dead leaves as they hibernate, to avoid being seen.

Tortoiseshell butterfly Adult butterflies hibernate from October onward, in garden sheds, hollow trees, caves, or roof eaves. They wake up in spring or even before if the weather is warm.

Ladybugs Some ladybugs spend the winter in large groups, clustered on plant stems, under fallen leaves or tree bark. They may also hibernate inside houses, in the corners of windowpanes.

Color and camouflage

Insects use color to send a variety of messages or to conceal themselves from predators.

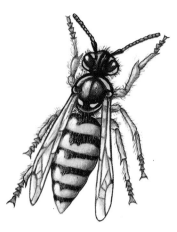

Warning colors In nature, combinations of red and black, or yellow and black, are used as warning colors. They warn birds that insects such as ladybugs taste terrible. Similarly, the colors warn that bees and wasps can inflict painful stings.

Wasp

Mimics Quite harmless insects, such as clearwing moths, hoverflies, bee flies, and some beetles mimic the warning colors of wasps, bees, and ladybugs. Predators are usually fooled and leave them alone.

Flash colors Some grasshoppers use both color and camouflage to great effect. At rest, their brown and green colors camouflage them among plants and twigs. If they are disturbed by a bird, they fly off, flashing brightly colored hind wings. Then, quite suddenly, they land again and disappear into the background. The confused bird is left searching for its prey.

Eyed hawk moth

Eyespots Some butterflies, moths, and their caterpillars have large, staring eyelike markings which are flashed to scare off birds. The birds are thought to mistake the eyes for those of one of their own enemies, for example, a cat.

Frightening face The green and brown coloring of the puss moth caterpillar camouflages it among willow and poplar leaves. But if something disturbs it, it rears up, flashing false eyes and lashing out with its tentaclelike hind legs. If this doesn't work, it squirts formic acid at its attacker.

Camouflage Many insects camouflage themselves by looking like something else, for example, twigs, thorns, leaves, or flowers. With their long, slender bodies, stick insects can hold themselves still and look exactly like the twigs they are resting on. They will even sway as if they are twigs being blown by a breeze. Their eggs, too, are camouflaged to look like plant seeds.

Industrial coloring Peppered moths in Britain and Europe have evolved two forms of camouflage to suit their particular environments. In country areas, they are light and speckled to hide them against lichen-covered tree trunks. But in industrialized areas, they have evolved a darker coloring to match soot-blackened tree trunks.

Other insects have also undergone this process, which is called industrial melanism. There are darker forms of many moths and grasshoppers.

Camouflage check

Make a small collection of insects from a bush or tree in your garden, using an umbrella or piece of white paper, as described on page 9. Look at the insects carefully. Make a comparison of those which use color to camouflage themselves and those which use bright colors to advertise their presence and deter predators.

More things to do

Studying insects

The study of insects is called entomology. One of the best ways to begin studying insects is to make your own collection. Some of the equipment you will need is listed on page 9. You can use a pooter to collect small insects from bark, twigs, and leaves. Place the long tube over the insect and suck on the short tube to capture the insect inside the jar.

You could also use a pitfall trap to catch insects. Bury a jam jar up to its neck in soil. Balance a flat piece of stone or slate on two pebbles above it. Bait the trap with meat, cheese, or jam and leave it overnight.

Take the insects home in plastic boxes, with a small leaf or piece of moss for them to cling to. Then transfer them to glass jars or see-through plastic containers so you can study them. When you catch the insects, note what they are feeding on and whether they prefer sunny or shady places. Try to keep them in conditions as close to their natural habitat as possible.

Only collect insects from your garden and don't take any more than you really need. Handle them with great care – they are very fragile. Release them back into the wild when you have finished studying their behavior and appearance. If you want to look at larger insect collections, pay a visit to your local museum.

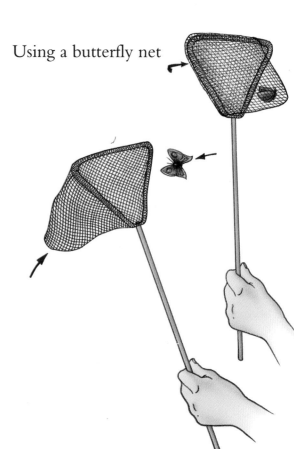

A butterfly net is useful for catching flying insects in meadows or around hedges. If you buy a net make sure it is light and strong, with a handle about 12 inches long so it is easy to control. Using a net properly takes a bit of practice. Sweep the net after the insect, or toward it. If you catch it, turn the handle so that the bag of the net folds over the frame, trapping the insect inside it. Do not continue sweeping the net back and forth as you will damage the insect you have caught.

Sketching insects

A quick sketch of an insect makes an excellent record, especially if you haven't got a camera. Sketch the insect in your notebook. It doesn't have to be a masterpiece! Draw ovals for the three parts of its body, then add antennae and legs, followed by wings if it has any. Note down its color, any special markings or features, and where and when you saw it. You can then look it up in your field guide later.

Making mini-habitats

A good way of watching insects is to create some mini-habitats for them in your garden. If you pile up some logs in a corner of the garden and leave them there, they will attract a range of insects which you can then observe closely.

Another idea is to lay a paving slab flat on the ground. This creates a warm, humid environment which is ideal for many different insects. Keep a note of the insects which use your mini-habitats throughout the year.

Attracting moths

Moths are attracted to lights – you have probably seen them crashing into windowpanes at night or flying around light bulbs. To study them more closely, hang a white bed sheet over the clothesline and shine a flashlight onto the sheet. You could even shine a strong reading lamp from the window onto the sheet. You will then get moths around the lamp as well as on the sheet.

Another way of attracting moths is to "sugar"a tree trunk. The best time to do this is at nightfall on a warm, calm night. Paint a tree trunk with some molasses and wait for the moths to arrive. If you don't have a tree in your garden, hang up an old cloth daubed with molasses. It will be just as effective.

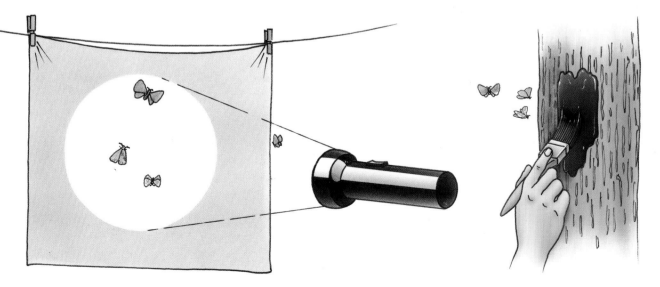

Index

PRINTED IN BELGIUM BY
proost
INTERNATIONAL BOOK PRODUCTION